A Hole Is a Great Home

by Bill Roberts

Illustrated by Jason Wolff

HAMPTON-BROWN

Hello, mole.
Pardon me.
May I poke my nose
in your home?

It looks like you like to dig.
That's why a hole is a
great home for a mole.

Hello, squirrel.
Pardon me.
May I poke my nose
in your home?

It looks like you go to
sleep in the winter.
That's why a hole is a
great home for a squirrel.

Hello, spider.
Pardon me.
May I poke my nose
in your home?

It looks like you wait and
then jump out to get bugs!
That's why a hole is a
great home for a spider.

Hello, woodpecker.
Pardon me.
May I poke my nose
in your home?

It looks like you need a
good nest for your eggs.
That's why a hole is a
great home for a woodpecker.

Hello, prairie dog.
Pardon me.
May I poke my nose
in your home?

It looks like you need lots
of rooms to live in.
That's why a hole is a
great home for a prairie dog.

Hello, rabbit.
Pardon me.
May I poke my nose
in your home?

It looks like you hate to get wet.
That's why a hole is a
great home for a rabbit.

Hello, dog.
Pardon me.
Where are you off to?

Why are you digging that hole?
A hole isn't a good home
for a dog, is it?

Nope, but it's a great home
for a bone!